TRINIDAD·TOBAGO

The author (right), when he was U.S. ambassador to Trinidad and Tobago, with the prime minister, Dr. Eric Williams (center), and Kamaluddin Mohammed, then minister of external affairs (left)

TRINIDAD·TOBAGO

Franklin Watts, Inc.
New York, 1975

◄A First Book►

ANTHONY D. MARSHALL

All photographs except the frontispiece
by Anthony D. Marshall

Map by Danmark & Michaels

Cover design by Jim Santiago

Library of Congress Cataloging in Publication Data

Marshall, Anthony D
   Trinidad-Tobago.

   (A First book)
   Bibliography: p.
   Includes index.
   SUMMARY: Introduces the geography, history,
government, economy, plants and animals, culture, and people of these two Caribbean islands
off the coast of Venezuela.
   1. Trinidad and Tobago—Juvenile literature.
[1. Trinidad and Tobago] I. Title.
P2119.M37   972.9′83   75–5527
ISBN 0–531–00835–5

CONTENTS

To my mother

TRINIDAD·TOBAGO

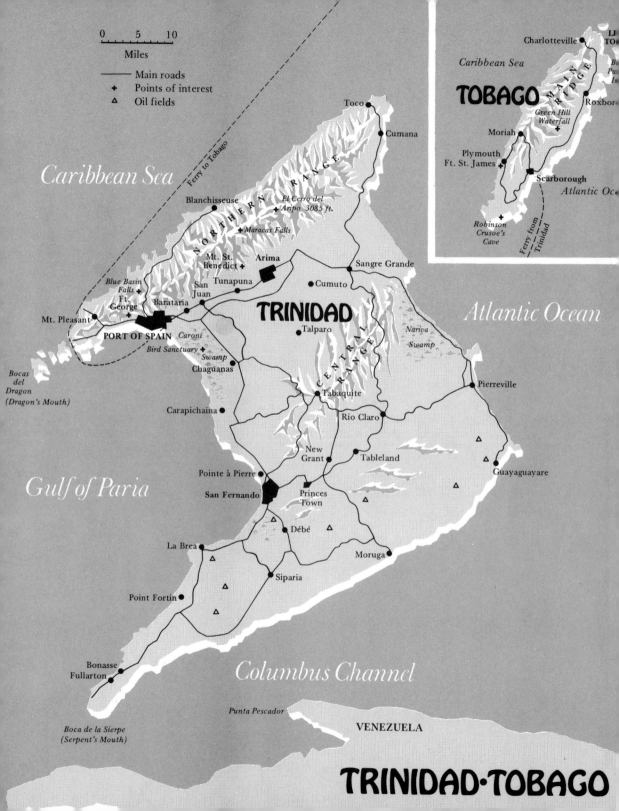

0   5   10
Miles
——— Main roads
+ Points of interest
△ Oil fields

Caribbean Sea

Ferry to Tobago

TOBAGO

Caribbean Sea

Charlotteville

Roxbor—

*Green Hill
Waterfall* +

Moriah

Plymouth
Ft. St. James +

Scarborough

Atlantic Oc—

*Robinson
Crusoe's
Cave* +

Ferry from Trinidad

Toco

Cumana

NORTHERN RANGE

Blanchisseuse

*El Cerro del
Aripo 3085 ft.* +

Maracas Falls +

Mt. St.
Benedict +   **Arima**

Sangre Grande

*Blue Basin
Falls* +

San
Juan   Tunapuna

Cumuto

Ft.
George +   Barataria

Mt. Pleasant +

PORT OF SPAIN   *Caroni*

TRINIDAD

Talparo

*Nariva
Swamp*

Atlantic Ocean

Bird Sanctuary +

Swamp

Chaguanas

*Bocas
del
Dragon
(Dragon's
Mouth)*

Tabaquite

CENTRAL RANGE

Pierreville

Carapichaina

Rio Claro

Gulf of Paria

New
Grant

Tableland

△

△

Guayaguayare

Pointe à Pierre

San Fernando

Princes
Town

△

△

△

Débé   △

Moruga

La Brea

△

Siparia

△

Point Fortin

△

Bonasse
Fullarton

Columbus Channel

Punta Pescador

VENEZUELA

*Boca de la Sierpe
(Serpent's Mouth)*

TRINIDAD·TOBAGO

TRINIDAD AND TOBAGO, an independent country within the Commonwealth of Nations

Independence Date: August 31, 1962.
           Location: Trinidad: 10° 3′–10° 50′ N., 60° 55′–61° 53′ W.; Tobago: 11° 9′ N., 60° 40′ W.
              Area: Trinidad: 1,864 square miles; Tobago: 116 square miles.
           Capital: Port of Spain (110,000).
        Population: 1,100,000 (43 percent black, 40 percent East Indian, 1 percent white, 1 percent Chinese, 15 percent mixed and other races).
          Literacy: 82 percent; Language: English.
          Religion: Predominantly Christian (25 percent of the population are Hindus or Moslems).
        Government: Constitutional monarchy. Bicameral legislature (24-member Senate; 36-member House of Representatives). Head of State: governor general, appointed by H.M. Queen Elizabeth II on the advice of the prime minister of Trinidad and Tobago. Head of Government: Dr. Eric Eustace

ESSENTIAL FACTS

Williams (prime minister), elected, since independence, 1962– .

Economy: Imports: $768 million (1973); Exports: $684 million (1973); Per capita GDP: $885 (1971); Currency: TT $2.22 = U.S. $1 (1975).

Political Parties: People's National Movement (ruling); Democratic Labour Party; Liberal Party; People's Democratic Party; Action Committee of Dedicated Citizens.

NOTE: all dollar figures in this book are U.S. $.

5400 B.C.	
to 3200 B.C.	Excavations (1969) reveal man's presence in Trinidad.
ca. A.D. 1000	Siboneys (a pre-Arawak strain originating in Florida) believed to have been living in Tobago.
1498	Christopher Columbus discovered Trinidad.
1498	Christopher Columbus sighted Tobago.
1557	Don José de Oruña founded city of San José (now known as St. Joseph); it became the capital of Trinidad in 1584.
1592	Spanish attempt to colonize Trinidad.
1595	Sir Walter Raleigh discovered Pitch Lake at La Brea.
1632–1676	Dutch tried unsuccessfully six times to form a colony on Tobago.
1640	Dutch invaded Trinidad.
1700	Cocoa first introduced to Trinidad.
1763	Tobago ceded by the Treaty of Paris to the English.
1769	Scarborough became the capital of Tobago.
1783	Port of Spain became capital of Trinidad.
1783	Carnival begins in Trinidad.
1786	San Fernando founded (Trinidad's second-largest city).

HISTORICAL CHRONOLOGY

1797 Sir Ralph Abercromby, first British governor of Trinidad.

1802 Spain formally cedes Trinidad to the British.

1807 African slave trade abolished.

1808 Port of Spain destroyed by fire.

1820 Botanic Gardens in Port of Spain begun by D. Lockhart.

1834 Slavery abolished in British Empire. Population of Trinidad at the Emancipation was 43,678: 3,632 whites, 18,627 free colored people, 20,657 slaves, and 762 aborigines.

1845 Immigration from India introduced for first time.

1850 First newspaper, *San Fernando Gazette,* started.

1851 First public library opened.

1866 First producing oil well drilled.

1889 Tobago annexed to Trinidad as one united colony.

1900 Venezuelan attempt to invade Trinidad.

1909 Sir William Ingram imported forty-eight greater birds of paradise to Little Tobago Island.

1937 Carlton Ford forms the first steel band.

1937 Labor riots in Fyzabad, Trinidad: fourteen killed, forty-four wounded.

1941 United States establishes naval base and air base.

1953 Caroni Reserve (for scarlet ibis) created.

1956 People's National Movement (PNM), Dr. Eric Williams's party, born.

1957 Trinidad named capital of the West Indies Federation.

1958 West Indies Federal Election. West Indies Federal Parliament inaugurated.

1962 (August 31) Trinidad and Tobago became independent.

1970   State of Emergency declared (lifted in 1972).

1971   General election returns Dr. Eric Williams as prime minister.

1972   Sir Ellis Clarke named governor general (took office in February 1973).

1972   Caribbean heads of government conference at Chaguaramas, Trinidad; establishment of non-resident diplomatic representation with Cuba.

1974   Dr. Eric Williams, prime minister, visits France; the People's Republic of China; and New York, where he attended the United Nations University Council meetings.

1975   Dr. Williams's trips abroad included Japan, China, Indonesia, and the United States.

*A Carnival steel band
playing in Tobago*

1 Carnival *is* Trinidad and Tobago. It is the land where the steel band, the calypso, and the limbo were born. Year-round the sound of the big metal drums can be heard, in towns and in the hills, their high-decibeled cacophony strangely harmonized by xylophonic precision. Once the steel band was only just discarded steel drums from oil refineries hammered and tuned into instruments; but now drums and percussion instruments have been added, and women, who were excluded ten years ago, play as well.

Carnival officially begins at five in the morning two days before Ash Wednesday with "J'Ouvert" or "Juve" (*Jour est Ouvert,* or "day opens"). This is a parade, with little organization, of thousands of people in bands, thronging through the choked streets, "jumping-with-it-Man," for those who find their way through Independence Square, passing the mayor's reviewing box. "J'Ouvert" is the time for the satirical and comical, for those who wish to put on rags and shuffle—or jump-up—through the town. It is the time for *mas':* the time for wearing a mask, carrying a placard with catchy political slogans. A time for old clothes and fun.

For those who wish, or can, the point is to stay up from "J'Ouvert" until midnight of the second day. Some have been up much longer, feverishly performing last-minute tasks on

CARNIVAL

their own or others' costumes. A bit of Trinidadian rum from time to time to keep one's spirits—or body—up helps.

The day before Ash Wednesday is the big day, the day of the passing of the bands. A day to forget the past, be happy with the moment, be unified today by the spirit of Carnival. Tomorrow, preparation for another year of Carnival begins all over again.

How did it all begin and what is it all about? The essential ingredients that make up Carnival are the bands, steel bands, and calypso.

Calypso singers or calypsonians poke fun at individuals, criticize government, laugh at serious situations. Their themes can be intellectual and constructive or abusive and vulgar; the latter is more regularly appreciated, though criticized. Calypsonians let off steam at Carnival.

There are some very good calypsos and calypsonians. Competition to be top calypsonian is fierce. Contenders for the calypso title in 1972 included Chalkdust, Lord Pretender, Lord Relator, Lord Kitchener, and—the winner—Mighty Sparrow, who took the title from the Mighty Duke, who had held it for four years. Mighty Sparrow's winning calypsos were "Rope" and "Drunk and Disorderly." "Rope," a road march, begins with the words "Time to unite"—an expression of the search for identity. Chalkdust, however, won top honors at Trinidad's Tenth Independence Anniversary celebrations with "Ten Years Old." The Mighty Sparrow won again in 1973.

Before Carnival, tents are set up by calypsonians. These so-called tents are, in fact, tents in name only; calypsonians, under the auspices of a group or organization, under a stucco or tin roof, offer nightly previews to the public of both their wit and their versatility. When a noted public or private citizen enters the tent, the calypsonian sings an impromptu verbal attack on the individual's weaknesses. Puns are often a part of a calypso, ridicule an ever-present feature.

A distinction must be made between a steel band and the masque (pronounced *mas'*) band. The Carnival's basic structural unit is the masque band, *masque* meaning that the band wears costumes on a theme from history, both modern and ancient; tribes and people of other lands; or a fantasy. There are also the traditional forms: the devils, demons, wild Indians, minstrels, robbers, bats, and clowns. The popular band is that of wild Indians: red, blue, or black, identified by the color of their costumes. The Red and Blue Indians were supposed to have come from Venezuela; the Black, from Africa. A Carnival masque band is a group of masqueraders numbering from several hundred to as many as four thousand who participate jointly in a Carnival theme. There are often well over one hundred bands vying for the title of best band.

In all their splendor, a dazzling panorama of moving color, bands pulsate their way through the streets, along the Savannah, up to the grandstand which is packed with everybody who is not participating, who is not "jumping up" with a band. The bands pass and the victor is chosen, as are the king and queen. In 1972 the winning band's theme was taken from the Anansi stories, West Indian folktales; the same band had won the year before with a fantasy theme built around Buccoo Reef, located off Tobago.

Perhaps the oldest (about 1860) traditional masque is the "neg jade," (*nègre jardin* or "garden negroes"), in which tight-fitting satin or velvet short trousers are worn with an embroidered shirt with a "fol," or heart-shaped panel of cloth hanging over the wearer's chest, decorated with rhinestones, mirrors, and swansdown. Rope sandals and a paper hat or crown, also elaborately decorated, complete the costume.

Going back a few years, in 1966, some of the outstanding bands included "Playing Cards" (375 participants); "Crete around 1500 B.C." (700); "Asia: B.C.–A.D." (1,000); "Snow Kingdom" (500), a fantasy of color and design emphasizing the shapes of snow crystals and all the colors of the rainbow; "Splendour among the Himalayas" (2,700); and "Dogs in Their Splendor" (800), with masqueradors wearing dog headpieces of all sizes and types and activities: at racing events, in police work, and in dog's attraction to the lamppost! One of the biggest bands ever was "U.S. Armed Forces in Hawaii" (4,000), in 1967.

The costumes that are created for Carnival are true works of inventive art. Harnessed into a rainbow-colored costume, decorated carefully with light-reflecting tinsel or sprayed surfaces, the wearer bears the weight with professional pride. The weeks that have gone into the production of the costumes are preceded by a year—or more—of research and design. Individuals pay from $75 to $300 or more for their costumes, while costumes of the principals soar to a much higher price.

A kitchen of "pans" or steel drums became a symphony of sound with the creation of the steel band. Carlton Ford, a Trinidadian, is said to have formed the Alexander Ragtime Band in 1937 in Port of Spain as *the* first steel band. Today there are many steel bands in Trinidad and Tobago, and the competition is fierce to be Carnival's winner. The pans are cut to different sizes to provide tonal values; the pans are then sectioned off by professional tuners to provide the notes. When the big day comes, and thousands have turned out for the finalist competition on the great Savannah in Port of Spain,

*Carnival costumes are
true works of inventive art.*

each steel band plays without following a score. Adaptations of classical music, such as Dvořák's *New World* Symphony, are rendered in metallic harmony. But most popular are the locally composed tunes that roar to a crescendo, stop with a thundering dramatic silence, and then return with deafening intensity. The crowd cheers.

Carnival "atmosphere" appears even in the church. In April 1972, the Cathedral of the Holy Trinity held a service that included a snappy, bouncy, gay "Calypso Carol." Military marches played by the Police Band for parades and reviews include calypso tunes and the calypso beat. Even in agriculture, a new crossbreed of cattle has been named Buffalypso.

Carnival's history in Trinidad goes back some two hundred years. Carnival, which began in Trinidad in 1783, under French immigrant influence, has changed its social form three times. First in 1833, after emancipation, when Carnival was discouraged and became increasingly disreputable. Then about 1863, the "Jamett" Carnival prevailed, or the Carnival of the "underworld." After harvesting the sugar, cane stalks were lit (*cannes brûlées*) and it became the vogue to parade through the streets with lighted cane torches on Sunday night preceding Carnival. After the so-called Canboulay Riot in 1881, such revelry was not allowed until Monday ("J'Ouvert") morning. The last change came in 1890, when Carnival began to take its present form.

While today Carnival spirit pervades Trinidad every day of the year, it warms up after Christmas with jump-ups—parties at which one bounces about until fatigued—with the repetitive rhythm of the melodic pans of steel bands, crescendoing, retreating a fraction, then coming at you again like a giant noise wave. It permeates you. You find yourself dreaming the beat of the big steel drums once your head is finally on a pillow.

2 The islands of Trinidad and Tobago, at their nearest point, are separated from Venezuela by only seven miles of sea. Geologically, the islands are part of Venezuela. Most of the flora and fauna are identical to Venezuela's, and so is the climate—in Trinidad. In Tobago, twenty-one miles from Trinidad, the trade winds are refreshing, and one frequently finds a cloudless day for snorkeling off Buccoo Reef while Port of Spain is experiencing a torrent of rain.

Trinidad (1,864 square miles) is roughly rectangular in shape, about 50 miles from north to south and 37 miles east to west. It has three mountain ranges. The Northern and Southern ranges run across the island, east to west; the Central Range crosses the island diagonally. The highest point is El Cerro del Aripo (3,085 feet). The entire southern coast is a cliff formation, constantly eroded by the sea. Both the eastern and western coasts contain swampland. The east coastline is a stretch of white beach, bordered by palms far inland, lapped by repeating rows of waves, edging up to fishing villages. On the west, however, Venezuela's Orinoco River silts up the Gulf of Paria, that body of water bracketed by the Dragon's Mouth on the north and the Serpent's Mouth on the south, separating Trinidad from Venezuela. In spite of the romance attached to Trinidad as a Caribbean island alive with Carnival, there are no good, easily accessible

GEOGRAPHY, FLORA, AND FAUNA

View of one of Trinidad's palm-bordered beaches

beaches on the island. Tobago, on the other hand, still remains a tropical paradise, often thought to be the setting of Defoe's *Robinson Crusoe,* where good beaches abound. Tobago (116 square miles) is 26 miles long and 7½ miles wide. A rugged ridge cuts down the center of the island, its highest point being 1,890 feet.

Trinidad and Tobago are tropical islands. The climate is tropical, with an average temperature of 77° F. in January and 84° F. during the day and 74° F. at night in May. However, July and August are climatically the most unpleasant months, with high humidity (average annual humidity at 8 A.M. is 81 percent, but it goes up to 95 percent in August), and the height of the rainy season. There are two seasons: the dry season from January to May and the wet season from June to December. Although not in the normal hurricane path (the exception, Flora on September 30, 1963, inflicted severe damage, particularly in Tobago, where 75 percent of the cocoa crop was destroyed), there are occasionally severe storms. Accompanying the storms is heavy rain; average rainfall for northeastern Trinidad is 120 inches, for the rest of the island 50 inches or more. Tobago's average is 56 inches per year, although the rains fall mostly along the mountain range.

The Trinidad and Tobago government is most conscious of the value and preservation of its land and what grows and lives on it. The government has created eleven nature reserves (1,611.5 acres) and thirteen wildlife sanctuaries (40,750 acres). In addition, there are thirty-five forest reserves (324,812 acres) in Trinidad and one (9,776 acres) in Tobago, out of a total of 570,000 acres of forest land surface (45 percent of the land surface). The reservation of lands for forest reserves started in 1901 and was completed in 1961.

Forest resources of Trinidad and Tobago produce approximately half of its timber needs. Timber, in Trinidad and Tobago, is used for the construction of houses. Some woods particularly adaptable for this purpose are cedar, yellow and pink poui, and mahoe. Teak, mahogany, cedar, and saman are used in furniture making; other woods are used for flooring and for boat building.

The national flower is the chaconia. Other common flowering shrubs include ixora, poinsettia, thunbergia, oleander, anthurium, bougainvillea, red ginger, and hibiscus; and there are handsome flowering trees, such as the frangipani, jacaranda, and poinciana (also known as the flamboyant or flame tree).

The flora of Trinidad and Tobago consists of a wide variety of plants, ferns, and flowers, including orchids, many-shaped and some named after insects. The most common orchids are yellow bee, cedros bee, butterfly, scorpion, and jack-spaniard; also often found are the monkey, goblet, lamb's tail, and virgin orchids. Crotons, handsome and popular shrubs, were first brought to the West Indies in 1840; they were first observed on the Moluccan Islands in Malaya in the fifteenth century. There are over two hundred varieties in Trinidad. Crotons stand as high as small trees. The strong leaves are generally a green-yellow or russet-yellow and have a glossy plastic look about them. They are found in most gardens, either as hedges or windbreaks. While the croton sheds old leaves, it is always full and makes an attractive background for smaller bushes or

A product of Trinidad's forests,
the breadfruit is
prepared in a number of ways.

flowers. The croton produces flowers of both sexes on the same plant. The roots have been used as medicine and croton oil is used for coughs.

As for the fauna of the country, there are 108 species of mammals, 324 species of birds, 37 snakes and 18 lizards, 25 amphibians, and 617 butterflies.

Let us start with the reptiles. There are only three poisonous snakes: the fer-de-lance, bushmaster, and coral (two kinds). The fer-de-lance is nocturnal and lives in the high woods and river valleys. Its bite produces great pain and swelling, and snake-bite serum should be used immediately. The bushmaster finds its home in deep forests where it hunts jungle rats and other rodents. The bushmaster's poison attacks the blood vessels; the victim dies from massive internal bleeding. The common coral snake is never longer than twelve inches and is often found in town gardens. This nocturnal snake has a potent poison, but people are unlikely to be bitten except perhaps between their fingers or toes. The large coral snake grows to fifty-two inches; it eats other snakes and worms and is usually found in cocoa plantations. Its poison attacks the nervous system of its victim. The most beautiful nonpoisonous snake of Trinidad and Tobago is the Laura or parrot snake, a bright emerald or leaf green, growing up to six feet in length. It is sometimes called the green horsewhip because of its slimness. It eats lizards, tree frogs, and occasionally young birds or bird eggs.

The wood slave, a lizard that is a member of the gecko family, is the only lizard in Trinidad with a voice. It can sometimes be heard, "kek kek kekkek," hunting for spiders and cockroaches in the beams of a roof. It is an unattractive, seven-inch-long thing, usually a gold-brown, but able to turn into a pale cream color, with no eyelids and bulging eyes. Other lizards include the matte (the largest, growing up to three and one-half feet); the garden lizard, welcome around the house, as it eats insects; the iguana, becoming scarce, since it is eaten by people who find it a tasty dish; the Mabouia, a gecko that lives in houses and catches moths and other insects; and the Polycrus or "twenty-four hours," the superstition (untrue) being that if it lands and stays on a victim for twenty-four hours, the victim dies. Actually, it makes a very good eighteen-inch-long pet —for those who like lizards as pets.

Mention must be made of the turtles of Trinidad and Tobago. The ten-inch-long galap is best known. It lives in freshwater swamps, rivers, and ponds. The leatherback sea turtle gets its name from its skin, which is leathery, instead of hard and bony as usually expected. It is the world's largest turtle, growing up to six feet in length and weighing up to 1,450 pounds. The green sea turtle is just somewhat smaller than the leatherback turtle. In May and June the leatherback comes up on the beaches of Trinidad to lay its eggs; but its future is endangered, because the eggs are too often collected by people for food, and the turtles themselves snared in wire. The leatherbacks are not protected by the government. In the moonlight, the waves lapping up on the two-mile length of Matura Beach on Trinidad's northeastern coast, a giant female turtle lumbers up from the water's edge to the sand near the mangroves. The female digs a three-foot-deep nest in the sand for her 150 eggs and is lucky if she is not surprised by poachers ready to hack her up for meat, leaving her shell a skeleton on the beach, her nest hole empty. Carefully, instinctively, the turtle covers the hole again with sand, and waddles back to her home in the sea.

The alligator also lives in Trinidad. There are a host of frogs—frogs that live entirely underwater, on trees, in swamps.

Frogs that "fly," change from golden-brown to dead white, are poisonous to dogs, and one that has a call that sounds like "pung-la-la." One of the most interesting frogs of Trinidad is the golden tree frog, found on the summit of El Tucuche, and nowhere else in the world. There are eighteen bat families in the world, nine of which are found in Trinidad and Tobago. There are more than sixty species of bats in Trinidad and Tobago: insect-feeders, fruit-eaters, nectar-drinkers, carnivorous bats, and purely sanguivorous (blood-feeding) bats. They live in caves, hollow trees, in roofs of houses, beneath leaves of fruit trees. Bats are helpful creatures. By feeding on insects, they help control them. They are useful for the work they do in the pollination and seed dispersal of plants, and for the guano that they deposit in caves, which is used as a fertilizer. The only bat found in caves that transmits rabies is the *Desmodus rotundas.*

The scorpion is found quite frequently in Trinidad, even in gardens of houses in Port of Spain. If you are bitten, you should cut out the bite, suck out the poison from the wound, and then take large doses of ammonia or sugar internally. Of the two hundred species of the family, Scorpiondias, there are seven in Trinidad and three in Tobago. However, the *Tityus trinitalis pocock,* most common in Port of Spain, is the most common scorpion in both Trinidad and Tobago. It is frequently found under coconut husks, logs and forest debris, in forests, sugarcane fields, banana, cocoa and coconut plantations, and in houses. This species is responsible for most of the deaths from scorpion bites, about six each year. Scorpions are related to spiders, ticks, and mites. They live on insects, cockroaches, and crickets. Females give birth to about thirty young. A scorpion takes five years to attain its full length; it has several pairs of eyes located on its back and is said to be most susceptible to music.

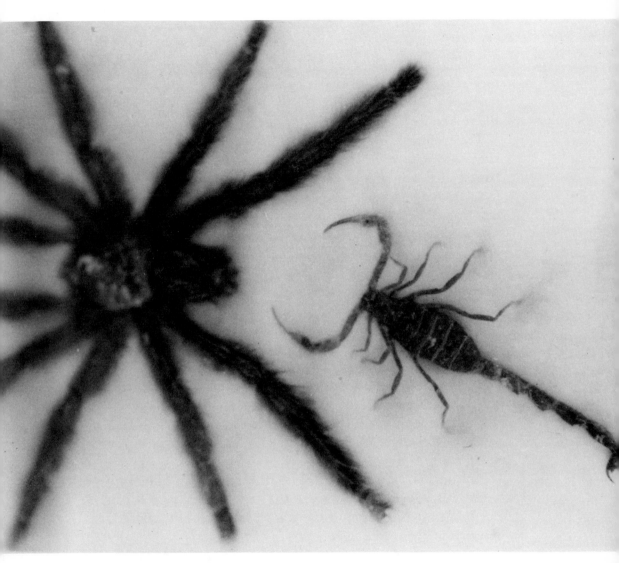

*Scorpions and spiders are
found throughout the islands.*

A large, hairy native spider is often mistaken for the tarantula; there are, however, no tarantulas in Trinidad.

The humorous-looking lantern fly (*Prictus serratus*) is five inches long and looks like a hippopotamus—with wings. It is fairly rare in Trinidad but is easily identifiable, even at night, when it emits phosphorescent bubbles.

The mammals of Trinidad and Tobago include the manicou, also known as the opossum. There are three species. The largest is the midnight manicou; it feeds on crabs and river fish. Then there is the mouse opossum and the brown-colored manicou. The mouse opossum and brown-colored manicou are eaten, either stewed or curried. However, the animals have glands that must be removed before cooking, for they contain an acid that creates an unpleasant skunklike odor when the animals are alive, and bitter taste if cooked. Manicous usually live in mango or pommerac trees.

The mongoose was brought to Trinidad from India to help eradicate the fer-de-lance snake that frequented the sugar plantations. While the mongoose is usually the winner in a fight with a fer-de-lance, if it happens to be bitten it eats a particular forest leaf that cures it of the poison, according to tradition. The mongoose is quite common in Trinidad and Tobago, much to the anger of the farmer who loses chickens to the sly mongoose.

The agouti, however, is faced with extinction. The agouti is a nervous, alert, tricky rodent that runs on a jagged course, nearly always returning to the place from which it started. It is hunted for the frying dish.

Other mammals include deer, lappe, quenk, red howler and Trinidadian Capuchin monkeys, tatou (an armadillo), anteaters, porcupines, tayras, squirrels, wildcat (rare), tiger cat, and matapel.

Now, the birds. Most magnificent are the scarlet ibis, found nesting in the Caroni Swamp Forest Reserve. The swamp itself is 260 square miles. The reserve, created in 1936, totals 7,900 acres. In 1953, 337 acres were set aside as a sanctuary, mainly for scarlet ibis, which numbered 8,000 at that time. Extensions were made in later years, which have brought the sanctuary up to its present 494 acres, with a scarlet ibis population of about 10,000. A total of 138 species of birds have been recorded, including herons, ducks, egrets, and ospreys, as well as doves, orioles, and flycatchers. The vegetation of the sanctuary consists entirely of mangroves, growing up to eighty feet in height. On the submerged roots of the red mangrove grow the edible mangrove oysters, along with mussels, barnacles, hydroids, sponges, tunicates, and tube worms. Fiddler crabs and mangrove tree crabs are abundant, and the hairy and tree crabs are edible. Also found in the sanctuary are a number of edible fish: the grouper, tarpon, mullet, snapper, and catfish, as well as prawns. Some say that the scarlet ibis includes a red crab in its diet, accounting for its scarlet color.

There are eleven reserves and thirteen wildlife sanctuaries in Trinidad and Tobago. In the Northern Range Wildlife Sanctuary, above twenty-seven hundred feet in altitude, are found the band-tailed pigeon, the orange-billed nightingale-thrush, and the blue-capped tanager, all distinctly local. In Trinity Hills Wildlife Sanctuary, along the southern coast of Trinidad, thirty-one species of birds have been recorded. The two most interesting are the rare mountain quail dove and the paui, which was once thought to be extinct in Trinidad. The Saut D'Eau Island Sanctuary boasts Trinidad's only breeding colony of brown pelicans, although twenty-six other species have been recorded, including the chestnut-collared swift and the rare rufous-necked wood rail. The Soldado Rock Sanctuary is a

*The mountainous Northern Range
in Trinidad provides a home for
numerous birds and other wildlife.*

seabird colony with sooty terns and brown noddies. St. Giles Island Sanctuary prides itself on being one of the most important seabird breeding colonies in the southwestern West Indies, the magnificent frigate bird (or man-of-war) and the red-footed booby being the most special inhabitants.

In 1909 Sir William Ingram imported forty-eight greater birds of paradise from the Aru Islands near New Guinea, which he then freed on Little Tobago, now a sanctuary and usually called Bird of Paradise Island. It is one mile off the northeast coast of Tobago and is about 450 acres in size. Three more birds of paradise were added in 1912. The 1963 hurricane Flora did much to damage the island; the current bird of paradise population is estimated at only seven. The island is also the home of four species of bats, six lizards, one harmless snake, and fifty-eight species of other birds, including Audubon's Shearwaters, red-billed tropic birds, brown boobies, laughing gulls, and sooty, noddy, and bridled terns.

Among the striking birds on Tobago is the 14½-inch king-of-the-woods or Swainson's motmot, a metallic mixture of green and bronze with a brilliant azure-blue patch on the top of its head. It has a russet-brown breast with two little black dots in the center. The motmot's 8½-inch tail is one of its most interesting features: two long feathers with the shape of arrows. The cocorico (also known as the red-tailed guan or rufous-tailed chachalaca) is Tobago's "official" bird. Twenty inches long, it is slate-gray with a blue-green sheen and outer feathers tipped with bright chestnut, and a long tail.

Trinidad is often called the island of the hummingbird. Eighteen species exist in the world; sixteen have been recorded in Trinidad, the largest of which is the green-throated mango. Strangely, some species of hummingbirds are found in Trinidad that are not found in Tobago, and vice versa. However, all the

Trinidad species of hummingbirds are related to those found elsewhere in South or Central America, and to nearly all in Venezuela. All hummingbirds have some green coloring, either on the wings, head, throat, back, or tail plumage. The hummingbird most often seen is the common emerald, $3\frac{1}{2}$ to $3\frac{3}{4}$ inches in length; its upper parts are bronze-green with a brilliant iridescent emerald-green from chin to lower breast. It is found up to two thousand feet, and nests in frangipani trees, using large pieces of lichen and spiders' webs for the construction of its home.

3 Columbus discovered Trinidad on July 31, 1498, on his third voyage to the New World. While Arawaks, one group of Amerindians, inhabited Trinidad when Columbus first sighted the island, there is also evidence that Aruaca, Chayma, Tamanaco, and Cumanagote tribes inhabited the island. The Amerindians were agriculturalists, and ate cassava, as well as maize, sweet potato, and a number of fruits. They also cultivated cotton and tobacco. The Arawaks were an essentially peaceful people.

The Caribs, a warlike people who also lived on Trinidad, are nearly extinct today (a settlement of about three hundred Caribs lives on the Caribbean island of Dominica), although the queen of the Caribs, a fragile elderly woman, still lives in Arima, Trinidad.

Excavations by P. O'B. Harris, beginning in 1969 at Banwari Trace, just south of San Fernando, Trinidad, have revealed occupation over two thousand years, dating from about 5400 B.C. to 3200 B.C. Human beings have, therefore, been on Trinidad for some time. Artifacts from pre-ceramic sites of Banwari and nearby St. John's include projectile points, possible nose or ear ornaments and pins, dating from between 4200 and 4000 B.C. Edge grinders, grinders, hammerstones, mortars, milling stones, and pestles have also been found dating from 5000

COLUMBUS DISCOVERS TRINIDAD

B.C. The Trinidad edge grinder dates from 5300 B.C., and digs in Cerro Mangote, Panama (ca. 4860 B.C.), and Cabo Blanco and El Heneal, Venezuela (ca. 2450 B.C.), have turned up similar implements.

The first successful attempt to colonize Trinidad was made by the Spaniards in 1592. In spite of repeated attempts made by the French, Dutch, and English to wrest the island away from the Spaniards, it remained Spanish until 1802, when it was formally ceded to the British. In 1733 a census revealed that there were 162 male adults (of which only 28 were white) in Trinidad; this did not take into account Indians or slaves, who were not included in the census. The total revenue of the Spanish colony was only £48. By an act of 1807 the British Parliament stopped the importation of slaves into Trinidad, which at that time had a population of 31,478 (which was 11 percent white). This act extended to Tobago in 1814, which had a population of 16,520 (of which 13 percent was white). With the abolition of slavery throughout the British Empire in 1834, many liberated blacks left the sugar estates on which they had been working. This led, in 1854, to the importation of indentured laborers from India, which continued until 1915. Between 1845 and 1917 some 150,000 migrants entered Trinidad from China, Madeira, and India.

The first capital of Trinidad, San José (now known as St. Joseph), was established in 1584, near Port of Spain, the present capital. In 1595 San José was burned down by Sir Walter Raleigh, who was also responsible for having found the large natural asphalt pit in southern Trinidad that today produces 130,000 tons a year. On March 24, 1808, a fire, started in an outhouse in Port of Spain, destroyed seven-tenths of the town.

San Fernando, Trinidad's second-largest city and capital of the southern part of the island, was founded in 1786 when a grant of land was made to Isidore Vialva, who sold it to Jean Baptiste Jaillet, who, in turn, broke it into small lots which he sold. On May 1, 1818, San Fernando was destroyed by fire. Today it is a thriving community, surrounded by oil-processing plants and refineries, and industry.

Tobago was originally inhabited by the Siboneys, a pre-Arawak group of people who came from Florida. They are believed to have lived on the island before A.D. 1000. They were followed by the Arawaks and Caribs. Columbus sighted Tobago on August 14, 1498, although he did not land. Later the island was known as Tabacco, Tobacco, Tabc, and Tavago.

The island was uninhabited in 1632, when a company of Dutch merchants was sent to settle it. From 1632 to 1676 the Dutch made six tries to form a colony but were forcibly discouraged by Indians, Spaniards from Trinidad, or by the British and French. Pirates made Tobago their base during the first quarter of the eighteenth century. In 1763 Tobago was ceded by the Treaty of Paris to the British, who established the first formal colonial administration there. In 1770 John Paul Jones, a British subject who later became an American naval hero in the Revolution, visited the island and was arrested for ill-treating his ship's carpenter. A year earlier Scarborough had become the capital of Tobago, and it remains so today.

Tobago was captured by the French in 1781, retaken by the British in 1793, and became French again under the Treaty of Amiens in 1802, but remained so only until 1803, when the French surrendered it to the British without a fight. Tobago had actually been buffeted from one owner to another thirty-one times since Columbus had first claimed it for Spain. In 1889 Trinidad and Tobago were combined under one administration; eventually in 1898 the British made Tobago a ward of Trinidad.

*Ancient cannons still guard
Fort St. James in Tobago.*

Today about 43 percent of the population of Trinidad is of African descent, 40 percent from India, 1 percent European, 1 percent Chinese, with 15 percent mixed and other races. In Tobago the population is essentially of African descent. The near-equality in numbers of East Indians and blacks in Trinidad provides a quality both of strength and of friction for the country. The ethnological diversity of the island adds a dimension of culture not found elsewhere in the West Indies. The Indians are good merchants and good farmers. While Indians are to be found in government, it is the blacks who aspire most strongly to hold official government positions. Of those who are unemployed, the majority are black; but it is the Indians, not the blacks, who show the greater interest in enrollment in business or trade courses offered by the government. Therefore, signs of unrest due to unemployment have been more noticeable among the blacks; the blacks tend to be more openly critical than the East Indians, and the Indians less willing to express any criticism of government for fear of reactionary outbursts against their tangible interests. Thus, while this mixed society produces evident progress for Trinidad, it can also be the basis for future problems.

In 1958 the United Kingdom established the autonomous West Indies Federation, comprising Jamaica, Barbados, the Leeward and Windward Islands, and Trinidad and Tobago. Port of Spain was the federation's capital. However, in 1961 Jamaica withdrew from the federation; and in 1962, Trinidad and Tobago became fully independent and a member of the Commonwealth of Nations.

4 When Jamaica withdrew from the West Indies Federation in 1961, the federation fell apart. A constitutional conference, held in London in April 1962, paved the way for the independence of Trinidad and Tobago, and status in the Commonwealth of Nations on August 31 of that year. The Commonwealth is an association of nations and dependencies loosely joined by the common interest of having been a part of the British Empire.

The two major political parties, the People's National Movement (PNM) and the Democratic Labour Party (DLP), and the government of the United Kingdom agreed on the provisions of independence: that Trinidad and Tobago be a member of the British Commonwealth, with a governor general as the queen's representative, and a cabinet headed by the prime minister; that there be a Parliament of two houses: representatives and senators, as in the United States; and that the judicial system include a Court of Appeal with final appeal to the Judicial Committee of the Privy Council.

Parliament consists of a House of thirty-six members, elected to a five-year term, and a Senate of twenty-four members appointed by the governor general, some on the advice of the prime minister and others on advice of the leader of the opposition.

GOVERNMENT

Whitehall, the prime minister's office, faces the Savannah in Port of Spain.

Administratively, Trinidad and Tobago is divided into eight counties or thirty wards (Tobago is the thirtieth).

Number one man in Trinidad and Tobago is Dr. the Right Honorable Eric Eustace Williams, prime minister of Trinidad and Tobago since independence and also the minister of external affairs. All important decisions are made by him, on advice from his cabinet. His office, modest and spartanly furnished, is situated on the second floor of Whitehall, a wedding-cake-like, sparklingly white building facing the Savannah, bracketed between the impressive, almost Moroccan residence of the Catholic archbishop on one side and on the other by a private stone residence styled as a small castle with crenellated towers. An easy subject for cartoonists, Dr. Williams is never without his dark glasses or hearing aid.

Dr. Williams was born on September 25, 1911. In 1931 he entered St. Catherine's Society, Oxford University, to read modern history. He considers himself, and is, an intellectual, and has written a number of books. He is particularly fond of watching cricket, actively follows Carnival developments, initiated a Best Village Competition to revive folklore (mostly Carnival in nature) and instill a spirit of competition and unity. However, his overwhelming preoccupation is his political party (PNM) and manipulating the complexities of government.

Dr. Williams was awarded his doctoral degree for his thesis on "Economic Aspects of Abolition and Emancipation of Slavery in the British West Indies." From 1939 until 1947 he was a professor of social and political science at Howard University,

Celebrating San Fernando Day,
the founding of Trinidad's second city

*The police horse guard
on parade*

Washington, D.C.; and from 1943 to 1948, a consultant to the Anglo-American Caribbean Commission, Washington, D.C. In 1948, Dr. Williams returned to Trinidad as research secretary, Caribbean Commission, and later was deputy chairman, Caribbean Research Council of the Caribbean Commission, until 1955.

Dr. Eric Williams founded the PNM in 1956. In the elections of 1968, the PNM candidates won fifty-four of the eighty-six seats contested. However, in the elections of 1971, the opposition chose not to vote; the PNM therefore won all the seats, although this represented, so the opposition claims, only 28 percent of the vote. In July of 1972 two PNM senators left the PNM but chose to stay in the Senate and were officially recognized as the "opposition" by the governor general.

The first plank of the PNM platform in 1962 was the political education of the people. The second plank was nationhood; the third, morality in public affairs. The PNM gave emancipation to women, with equal rights on an equal footing with men in the political life of the country.

On September 29, 1972, Prime Minister Williams, as political leader of the PNM, spoke at the party's fourteenth annual convention. Among other statements, he said that "Trinidad and Tobago is a veritable oasis as compared with the deserts that have emerged in many parts of the world."

A Constitutional Reform Commission, under the chairmanship of Sir Hugh Wooding, chancellor of the University of the West Indies, researched the needs and wishes of the people of Trinidad and Tobago. The PNM, in October 1972, publicly advocated that Trinidad and Tobago become a republic but seek to remain within the Commonwealth.

Trinidad and Tobago experienced what is politely referred to as "the disturbances" in the spring of 1970, when a mutiny took place in the Regiment, Trinidad's then thousand-man army. The matter was resolved, with the help of the 3,500-man police force, and the Regiment was reduced in strength and brought under control. The Trinidad and Tobago Coast Guard (there is no navy) is comprised of four vessels, H.M.T.S. *Trinity, Courtland Bay, Chaguaramas,* and *Buccoo Reef,* each with a displacement of 98 tons and 103-foot length; in addition, there is an airplane.

5 Trinidad and Tobago was a member of the West Indies Federation during its life, 1958–61. This was an attempt to achieve solidarity in the Caribbean. Several other parries at some form of federation have been made subsequently. In 1972, St. Lucia, St. Vincent, and Grenada joined in declaring a free exchange and passage between the three Associated States. Also in 1972, a group of government and private citizens gathered in Tobago to declare the need for a federation of several Caribbean states, but excluding Jamaica for the time being. At the same time, Anguilla moved to sever its association with St. Kitts and Nevis.

Need for economic coordination of interests and efforts is realized, and a genuine attempt has been made through CARIFTA (Caribbean Free Trade Association), an organization created in 1968 to encourage the development of trans-Caribbean trade, through duty-free entry as well as by other incentives. One result of a conference of heads of Caribbean governments in Trinidad in October 1972 was the decision that CARIFTA should be changed into a Caribbean Common Market; in 1973 CARIFTA was replaced by CARICOM (the Caribbean Community). Because of shipping costs, transportation facilities, other economic factors involving raw materials and markets, or nationalistic jealousies, the development of CARICOM has not yet been the success

TRINIDAD, THE CARIBBEAN, AND THE WORLD

that each country, at least in theory, wishes it would be. However, Trinidad and Tobago has been working more and more together with Jamaica, Guyana, and Barbados, on both economic and political (joint statement regarding Cuba) issues.

Regarding Cuba, Dr. Eric Williams expressed his views in clear terms: Cuba cannot be denied its position in the Caribbean. He has frequently reiterated his position; and, on October 14, 1972, at the conclusion of the heads of Caribbean government conference in Port of Spain, it was declared by the governments of Trinidad and Tobago, Jamaica, Barbados, and Guyana that an early establishment of association with Cuba would be sought, economic or diplomatic, or both. Subsequently, nonresident ambassadors were appointed. In the same framework of association, Dr. Williams has commented on the subject of Puerto Rico (in his book *From Columbus to Castro*), saying, "Economic growth has been achieved, but national identity lost. What shall it profit a country if it gain the whole world and lose its own soul?"

Latin America is at Trinidad's doorstep. There are four Latin-American embassies in Port of Spain: Venezuela and Brazil, both with resident ambassadors, and Colombia and Argentina, with chargés. Trinidad and Tobago joined the Organization of American States (OAS) in 1967; it is also a member of the Economic Commission for Latin America (ECLA) and the Inter-American Development Bank (IADB). The OAS has a permanent representative in Port of Spain (as has the IADB) and has been instrumental in providing funds for feasibility studies.

Port of Spain, capital
of Trinidad and Tobago,
seen from the harbor

The OAS also, of course, acts as a forum for expression of views on a multitude of subjects. The attempt at Latin-American trade ties has been difficult, as Trinidad and Tobago's natural trade partners historically have been the United Kingdom (for the past two hundred years) and Canada, because of trade preferences. Jamaica has a high commissioner located in Port of Spain, who is also accredited to Venezuela, Barbados, Guyana, and the Associated States.

At the heads of Caribbean government conference in October 1972, it was decided that there be a coordination on inter-related questions of matters of the Law of the Sea, taking into account the needs of developing countries, including those not yet independent; and that a standing committee of ministers from all thirteen states participating in the conference would be established to develop regional cooperation in matters of common interest in foreign policy. One further, important statement was made at this conference: "To adopt all necessary measures to bring the exclusion of Commonwealth Caribbean countries from the Inter-American system to an end." A particular point was made regarding the exclusion of the non-independent states from the resources of the Inter-American Development Bank.

Trinidad and Tobago became a member of the United Nations in 1962. It is a member of the United Nations Industrial Development Organization (UNIDO). In addition, it has participated in the United Nations Conference on Trade and Development (UNCTAD). At the third UNCTAD meeting in Santiago, Chile,

The international diplomatic corps in Port of Spain, observing the National Day of Remembrance

in the spring of 1972, Trinidad and Tobago joined others in expressing their concern regarding their economic relations with (and particularly in obtaining concessions from) developed countries. Trinidad and Tobago is also a member of the United Nations University Council.

According to Prime Minister Williams, UN issues of particular concern to Trinidad and Tobago are: "the Law of the Sea, the movement against colonialism, the sanctions against the illegal regime in Rhodesia, the relentless opposition to the degradation of apartheid in South Africa, and the right of Cyprus to self-determination." Dr. Williams also said, in the same publication, that the three outstanding examples of Trinidad and Tobago's "international orientation and vision are: (1) the gradual and rational reintegration of Chaguaramas* into the national patrimony; (2) Switzerland's assistance to the Institute of International Relations on the initiative of the Government of Trinidad and Tobago; and (3) technical assistance from the Federal Republic of Germany in respect to the seed project at Chaguaramas."

Kamaluddin Mohammed, who was then the minister of External Affairs, enumerated the main features of Trinidad and Tobago's foreign trade policy in a 1972 speech. He stated that "over the years there has been a maintenance of the present preferential arrangements with the United Kingdom, particularly as regards agricultural exports, both because of the preponderance of these products in their total exports and because they affect the activities that generate most employment." He pointed out that a diversification of export markets exists "to

* Provided, by treaty, to the United States by
Great Britain as a U.S. naval base in World War II.

cushion the impact of the United Kingdom's entry into the European Common Market and of possible changes in the existing preferential arrangements." However, export substitution is necessary in order to "promote local production of a number of manufactured goods for domestic consumption and export," and that essential ingredients are "incentives for foreign investment as a supplement to local resources in the primary sector and in industry and tourism, together with Government's new policy of localization and joint participation" and "a policy of economic cooperation and regional integration, such as the Caribbean Free Trade Association."

This task is a difficult one to accomplish, to say the least. The United States is a natural market for Trinidadian goods, but *what* goods? And under what conditions? These questions are only answerable by patience, time, diligence, and hard work.

6 While oil is the dominant contributor to the financial welfare of the nation, the economy has developed and is developing in diverse directions.

U.S. business has a considerable investment of approximately $800 million in Trinidad and Tobago. While all figures are comparative, an interesting comparison lies with Africa. In January 1973, the United States had a $4 billion investment in Africa's forty-two countries. U.S. investment in Trinidad is, therefore, one-fifth of the total U.S. investment in Africa, or equal to the U.S. investment in either Nigeria or South Africa. Most of the U.S. dollars are in oil exploration, production, and refining by three American oil companies: Texaco, AMOCO (Standard Oil of Indiana), and Tesoro Petroleum (of Texas). Additionally, there are about sixty American companies that have manufacturing or assembly plants in Trinidad or an investment (including those in tourism) or an office or representation in Trinidad. The estimated resident American population in Trinidad and Tobago is nearly 1,800, including businessmen, students, missionaries, and clergy. There are as many as 100,000 Trinidadians and Tobagonians in the United States.

W. R. Grace and Co.'s Federation Chemicals Ltd., located at Point Lisas, opened in 1958 and produces nitrogen fertilizers. Liquid Carbonic West Indies Ltd., located at Savonetta, Trini-

ECONOMICS

dad, manufactures industrial gases, including bulk liquid nitrogen and oxygen. Alcoa Steamship Company, Inc., has a transit facility in Trinidad for the shipment of bauxite from Surinam. Sylvania and Westinghouse (Sunlight Industries Ltd.) both have assembly plants for U.S. products. Sylvania (General Telephone and Electronics Corp.) installed 25,000 telephone lines in Trinidad between 1961 and 1967, doubling the system at a cost of $15 million, financed by the Export-Import Bank. Sylvania now assembles radios and television sets in Trinidad.

Town and Country, a subsidiary of Highlander Ltd., New York, is one of the largest garment manufacturing factories in Trinidad, with about five hundred employees. Town and Country makes shirts and trousers. Its location is in Trincity, an industrial area on the outskirts of Port of Spain on the road to the airport. In all, there are as many as sixty garment manufacturers giving direct employment to seven thousand people. The Singer Company, Inc., has sales in Trinidad averaging 4,500 sewing machines a year, although one year it sold 7,200. In business in Port of Spain since 1910, Singer has 145 Trinidadian employees, one of whom has been with the company for forty-two years. Singer also assembles stoves and refrigerators (Admiral). Singer is involved in community matters, such as Junior Achievement, Folklore Festival, and the prime minister's Best Village Competition.

There are seven livestock feed mills in Trinidad. Two are American. Corn and soybean meal are the main products for sale on the local market. The Carlson Companies of Minneapolis, Minnesota, internationally known for their Gold Bond stamps, has had interests in Trinidad since 1964, including a Coca-Cola bottling facility, ice-cream plant, bakery, drug division, ship's chandlery, chicken processing operation, and a supermarket chain. In addition, it has an interest in and

QUALITY FEEDS

manages hotels in Tobago. The Myerson Tooth company of Cambridge, Massachusetts, introduced True-Blend teeth to the field of dentistry in 1937; they were the first artificial teeth to have a layer of transparent or translucent enamel, which greatly enhanced their appearance. In 1950 the Myerson Tooth Company started to manufacture teeth in Trinidad, where they now employ 150 Trinidadians. A number of other U.S. firms do business in Trinidad, and two American banks have offices on the island.

Trinidad's exports to the United States in 1972 amounted to $248.3 million. Its imports from the United States were $143.1 million (with industrial machinery and iron and steel accounting for a major portion of the purchases). Thus Trinidad's bilateral trade surplus with the United States (goods sold to the United States in excess of purchases) for 1972 was $105.2 million.

Sugar (along with tourism and oil) is the major money-earner for the country. In 1972 the United States purchased 10,962 metric tons of sugar from Trinidad and Tobago, the value of which was $1.9 million.

The Export-Import Bank of the United States provided a loan of $6.6 million in 1967 and $4.4 million in 1971 to the Trinidad and Tobago Electricity Commission for power-generating equipment from and services by General Electric. In 1972, the Export-Import Bank also provided part of the financing for commercial fishing trawlers for shrimp fishing.

Trinidadians working
at one of the
livestock feed mills

The U.S. embassy (prior to independence in 1962 it was a consulate general) in Port of Spain has a United States Information Service, which contains a library, and provides a book-presentation program (particularly to schools), and a film-lending facility; USIS counsels students wishing to go to the United States and conducts a varied program of cultural activities and events. There is no AID mission or Peace Corps in Trinidad and Tobago. The United States did present to Trinidad and Tobago a $30 million AID grant shortly after independence. Since 1970 the cultural affairs program has provided two American professors a year from the fields of telecommunications, sociology, business management, and engineering (food technology) to the University of the West Indies, St. Augustine campus, Trinidad.

During World War II, when Trinidad and Tobago was still a British colony, and when the United States needed naval and air bases, the British government provided, under the 1941 Leased Bases Agreement, considerable areas of land (particularly the Chaguaramas peninsula on the northern outskirts of Port of Spain) to the United States. In 1961 a new agreement was drawn up by the United States and the government of Trinidad and Tobago; in October 1971 the last military installation, a tracking station, was handed over to the government. Today no American in uniform is resident in Trinidad and Tobago. U.S. Navy ships pay frequent calls to Port of Spain; the ships and their crew are warmly received, with friendly basketball, soccer, and rifle matches arranged.

One facility that does still exist is OMEGA, a totally nonmilitary activity, on about a thousand acres of the Chaguaramas peninsula. OMEGA is a navigational system, replacing LORAN, effective within the earth's atmosphere, on the water, and underwater to within an accuracy of 400 yards. The system was de-

*Mechanized harvesting
of sugar cane*

vised at the instigation of the U.S. Navy and operated under its aegis until recently by five contract, civilian employees. OMEGA is now under the authority of the U.S. Coast Guard.

Agriculture accounts for 8 percent of the Gross Domestic Product (GDP) but employs 20 percent of the work force. Output increased from $52 million in 1962 (with independence) to $67 million in 1971. The sugar industry, first established in 1787 in Trinidad and by far the most important factor in molding the economy and destiny of Trinidad, was largely brought under national control and ownership during the late 1960s and early 1970s.

Since 1962 Caroni Ltd. (founded in 1937) has been the largest of six sugar companies, with 50,000 acres and 13,200 employees, manufacturing 90 percent of all sugar produced. Caroni has mechanized only a small portion of its harvesting with the purchase of six machines. Today, Caroni has four factories harvesting and processing the cane between January and late June. One $35,000 harvesting machine will do the work of eighty-eight people.

Food production for domestic consumption has increased, but development in other fields has tended to lag. Unemployment is a national problem, with more than 13 percent unemployed, but with a total of about 24 percent unemployed, unemployable, or underemployed. The country's average annual income is nearly $900. This compares most favorably with other developing countries of the world; for instance, in Africa, the average annual income per capita is $150.

While the raising of beef cattle has not been successful, due to inadequate pastureland and climate, that of breeding and dairy cattle has. By the end of 1972, 1,580 farms were developed by the government on 14,000 acres, under the Crown Lands Development Project. They consist of 260 dairy farms,

The buffalypso, a crossbreed
buffalo for beef, is ideally suited
to the Trinidadian climate.

70 pig farms, 65 tree crop farms, 1,160 food and vegetable crop farms, and 25 tobacco farms. The buffalypso, a crossbreed buffalo for beef, was produced after twenty years of research. A few water buffalo were imported into Trinidad in 1905 from India with the intention that they would replace the zebu or Brahman Indian cattle as work animals. The strains used in producing the buffalypso were the Murrah, Surti, Jaffarabadi, Nelli, and Bhadawari. The buffalypso is reddish brown in color with a tight coat, as opposed to the rough, irregular coat of the water buffalo.

The Ministry of Agriculture has been conducting experimental research with local fruit crops over the past ten years, particularly on mangoes, avocados, papaw, West Indian cherries, sapodillas, passion fruit, guavas, pomeracs, pineapples, mamee sapote, soursop, sugar apples, and governor plums. The citrus crops of grapefruits, oranges, and limes have been good, with increases over the previous years. Adequate and timely rainfall, wider use of fertilizers, fungicides, and weedicides have been the principal reasons for increased production.

Cocoa is the major agricultural export after sugar and its by-products: rum, molasses, and bagasse, used for fuel, cattle feed, and the manufacture of cellulose. While production has declined, the world market for cocoa has improved. From 1966 to 1971, cocoa production ranged from 9 to 13 million pounds annually, 98 percent of which was exported. Other main agricultural products are coffee, bananas, coconuts (copra), rice, poultry, dairy produce, and tobacco.

Trinidad's emphasis on forestation and reforestation deserves attention. The Forestry Division, Ministry of Agriculture, is responsible for managing about 45 percent of the total land area of Trinidad and Tobago. Its work ranges from conservation to the promotion of wider and more economic use of lumber, and includes training. Nearly seven thousand persons are involved in the timber business, either directly or indirectly as woodcutters, loggers, bullmen, truckers, loaders, sawmill workers, sawmill owners, and timber merchants. The country has sixty sawmills, one match factory, one parquet-tile flooring factory, two soft-drink case factories, as well as several small cabinet and joinery shops. The Forestry Division is reforesting forty thousand acres on the Northern Range of Trinidad that had been indiscriminately cleared by farmers for agriculture.

Manufacturing, including sugar refining, grew from a $66 million contribution to the total national output in 1962 to $156 million in 1971. Particular growth has taken place in the textile industry, food processing, building materials, and consumer appliance and automobile assembly industry components.

Angostura bitters is probably the most widely known export of Trinidad. The company that makes it, originally founded in Venezuela, was later moved to Trinidad, bringing with it the "secret formula" for Angostura bitters. In addition to "aromatic" bitters, the Angostura company concocts gin, vodka, amber rums, white rums, a Mokatia coffee liqueur, and methylated spirits.

The government of Trinidad and Tobago is the country's biggest employer, not only of civil servants, police and military, totaling eighty thousand, but in business. The government owns or controls at least sixteen companies, with investment in many others. It *controls,* for instance, 95 percent of the sugar industry. The largest work force is Caroni Ltd. (sugar plantation) with 13,200 workers, in which the government holds a 51 percent interest.

*A busy street, lined with
small businesses, in Port of Spain*

Many specialist institutions have assisted and are assisting in the economic development of the country. The Industrial Development Corporation (IDC) is one of these; the Development Finance Company is yet another. The Industrial Development Corporation was founded in 1959 "to stimulate, facilitate and undertake the development of industry in Trinidad and Tobago." The IDC has established seven industrial estates, containing 186 industrial sites ranging from one-half acre to five acres in size, and providing services such as industrial water, electric power, and telephone. In 1972, the country had 457 factories producing consumer goods, with a projected growth rate of 5 percent over the next fifteen years. The Small Business Unit of the IDC provides loans of up to $25,000 at between 5 percent and 6.5 percent interest per annum, repayable in eight years. A field of interest that has received considerable government attention is that of small enterprises (defined by the government as having a total investment of between $25,000 and $50,000) producing handicrafts, textiles and garments, batteries, food products, and building components. The IDC provides financing and space (in the industrial areas) for such businesses, if they require it. The Management and Productivity Centre assists starting businesses in management problems such as accounting, training courses, and sales concepts.

7 Oil flows through the financial veins of Trinidad and Tobago. Oil has brought foreign investment to Trinidad, developed some related (petrochemical) industry, provided Trinidad and Tobago with a favorable trade balance, and raised to a considerable degree the standard of living in the country. Oil is the present and very much the future of Trinidad. In addition to oil itself, there is natural gas. Government and business have concrete plans for the development and sale by 1977 of liquefied natural gas to the United States. The proven reserves, to date, are 612 million barrels of crude petroleum; liquefied natural gas production calls for 150 billion cubic feet per year. There are four major oil companies producing oil in Trinidad: Shell, and three American companies, Texaco, AMOCO (Standard Oil of Indiana), and Tesoro (of Texas). There are other oil companies or groups with concession interests, but they are not currently in production.

Oil production and refining have helped Trinidad and Tobago with its problems of unemployment and have helped counter the relatively slow development of privately controlled industries, and seasonal setbacks in sugar and other agricultural activities. Oil revenues have also helped the government provide benefits.

Texaco's desulfurization plant,
part of its petrochemical
investment in Trinidad

However, the quantity of oil being produced in Trinidad is very small relative to world production and the cost of production is high compared to the major oil-producing countries. For instance, the cost of Trinidadian oil is approximately three times more expensive than that of Venezuelan or ten times that of Middle East oil. The success of Trinidad's petroleum industry depends on the country's ability to market competitively and internationally. This will become even more important in the future, as the petroleum industry will be competing in the Free World energy market with other potential energy sources: tar-sand and shale oil, coal, nuclear power, and synthetic hydro-carbons.

Oil is not new to Trinidad. The first geological survey was undertaken in 1860. The first producing well was drilled on the Aripero Estate in 1866, producing sixty gallons of oil a week. However, the greatest advance has been in the past decade, at an accelerating pace.

Texaco acquired the Trinidad Oil Company Ltd. in 1956; by 1972 it had completed work on 96 exploration wells, 993 development wells, and 2,130 workovers. Texaco employs nearly eight thousand persons. Texaco produces about 80,000 barrels per day of crude oil and refines about 400,000 barrels per day at its Pointe-à-Pierre plant. Over the past decade Texaco has invested more than $300 million, including a desulfurization plant. Texaco's petrochemical production includes di-isobutylene, tetramer, nonene, benzene, toluene, xylene, cyclohexane, and normal paraffins. Cyclohexane is used in the synthetic fiber industry for the manufacture of nylon. Toluene is used for blending into gasoline. Normal paraffins (developed from kerosene) are used in the manufacture of a type of detergent that does not clog sewerage systems. Texaco has done much —and in many ways—to assist Trinidad and Tobago in its development. Texaco spends over $600,000 annually on education and training; it provides craft apprenticeship (machinery, electrical, instrumentation, bench fitting, and engine and pump fitting) annually for about fifty boys between the ages of fifteen and sixteen; about forty-five young men between seventeen and twenty-five are employed annually as student technicians (drilling, engineering, instrumentation, laboratory work, production, and storekeeping); and about fifteen to twenty-five young men each year are given a twelve-month course to prepare them for junior operators' positions at the refinery plants. Foreman, supervisory, and other training is also given, plus the award of twenty university scholarships per year. Texaco also has a very considerable interest in agricultural development: teak and Honduras pines afforestation, a sixty-acre food crops demonstration farm, endowment of a chair of agriculture at the University of the West Indies, and citrus plantations, as well as a dairy farm and beef cattle breeding unit.

AMOCO International Oil Company has a 1.5-million-acre offshore concession east of southern Trinidad, acquired in 1961, where low-sulfur, high-quality oil has been found. There are at present four offshore platforms, ranging up to twenty-five miles from Point Galeota, on the southeastern coast of Trinidad, where 16-inch pipes take the oil, store it, then repipe (42-inch pipes) it offshore again to ships for delivery in the United States. Production is about 50,000 barrels per day. Significant gas deposits were discovered in 1968 and 1969. A liquefaction plant is contemplated for Trinidad that will carry the solid gas to the United States in tankers. Due to the tremendous needs in the United States for gas, the development of liquefied natural gas in Trinidad, an eventual $700 million investment, is important not only to Trinidad but to the United States.

Tesoro Petroleum Corporation of San Antonio, Texas, was

joined by the government of Trinidad and Tobago in May 1969 to form the Trinidad-Tesoro Petroleum Company Ltd., which started operations in July 1970 with a thousand producing wells of 40,000 barrels per day. The concession area dates back to 1918, when the Trinidad Petroleum Development Company Ltd. was registered. All wells are onshore, except one, six miles from shore in seventy-foot-deep water. Tesoro also has an interest in citrus fruit and cocoa plantations and has a small but very efficient dairy farm.

The famous Pitch Lake at La Brea, in southern Trinidad, is said to have been used by Sir Walter Raleigh for his ships when he visited Trinidad. The ninety acres of pitch have been exploited since 1886. The asphalt production has averaged 130,000 tons a year.

Oil storage tanks at
Point Galeota, on Trinidad's
southeastern coast

8 A boatload of sixteen people climb up the steps of the beached glass-bottomed boat, using one of the two suspended outboard motors for support. Their blue snorkel masks dangle from their arms, one or two have flippers (which are unnecessary), most have on sneakers, as recommended to them, and nearly all wear bathing suits and sport a towel over their shoulders or about their neck. A crew of three release the hull from the sand and point the vessel seaward—toward Buccoo Reef.

Half an hour later, after alternately giraffing a look at the sea's bottom through the glass bottom and craning to catch a glimpse of Tobago's Pigeon Point—a living painting of tropical paradise—the boat's passengers arrive at the reef. The anchor is dropped, and the passengers reverse into standing-depth water, spit in their masks, fit them, and peer into an underwater wonderland, a rainbow of fish darting, nozzling, gliding about fantastic growths of coral.

Buccoo Reef is a chief, if not the chief, tourist attraction in Tobago. Tobago is a delightful, beautiful island with tropical vegetation and white sandy beaches. Only a small dent has been made by exploiters of tourism, developers of hotel complexes, and recreational facilities. This is good and bad. It is good for visitors seeking a nearly unspoiled isle—away from it all—where they can bask in the sun and fish. It is bad for income-hungry residents and the national coffers.

TOURISM

*Fishermen hauling in
their nets on Tobago*

Originally a sugar mill,
this tower is now a
hotel restaurant on Tobago.

The hotels that have taken root on the island are attractive and offer excellent facilities for the vacationer. There is good fishing year around, with better than even chances of hooking kingfish, wahoo, bonito, sailfish, marlin, dolphin, yellow-fin tuna, redfish, shark, grouper, deep-sea snapper, and barracuda. And the island's large number of bird species, both the nature birds and the imported ones, attract bird watchers.

In Trinidad the scarlet ibis are perhaps the most dramatic attraction for the tourist. But Trinidad is not a tourist's island; Tobago is. Trinidad has few tourist attractions, in the usual sense. There is only one small museum in Port of Spain, few restaurants (although some good Chinese ones) or nightclubs, and no accessible beaches with facilities. During Carnival, however, Trinidad is a technicolor panorama fulfilling the tourist's wildest fantasy wishes. While the government is interested in the promotion of tourism, development is still slow compared to other West Indian islands. There are plans to double the number of hotel rooms in the next five years.

9 It gets light before 6 A.M. in Trinidad. The dogs are barking, exciting each other into further exchanges; roosters before dawn had vied with the crickets, tree frogs, and night birds in breaking the silence of dark. A pack of stray dogs puts up a particular racket in a distant section of Port of Spain. Cars starting on the road, sixty thousand of them, all makes, many American; the squeak of brakes on the asphalt, which should jog the drivers into a sense of caution, but doesn't. The rate of accidents in the city, but especially on the road to the south, are increasing, as is the rate of mortalities. But the restlessness of a nation on the move, in a hurry to get there, becomes a fever when behind the wheel. Newspapers are being delivered: the *Trinidad Guardian* and *Express,* dailies; *Moko* and *The Bomb,* on Fridays; *Catholic Weekly,* Mondays, and the periodic PNM newspaper, the *Nation,* waiting on office desks for the start of business at 7:30 A.M. Car and home radios are tuned in for the 7 A.M. news, BBC and local. The day has started.

Green-tunicked schoolgirls walk or bus their way to school. The police horse guard and police dog squad start training before the heat of day. A few hardy people, intent on remaining so, jog a three-mile lap around the Savannah, a minister and judge among them. St. Andrews Golf Club, in Maraval,

ONE DAY

*This handsome house reflects
several of the cultures
that mingle in Trinidad.*

is visited by enthusiasts preferring morning to evening sport. A morning drizzle falls on the seventh tee, but then draws back to the hills above Port of Spain; the television antennae on the mountaintop become visible. The sun rises, sparkling over the harbor, illuminating the Gulf of Paria. You can see Pointe-à-Pierre, nearly thirty miles away, the oil refinery, and huge tankers gliding toward land.

Some factories have been open all night, some on early two-a-day shifts. The oil continues to flow through the pipes, and men have to be there to supervise the work. Chickens scatter up dust in a village distant from the capital as farmers start for work in the cane fields, the farms, the factories clustered about Port of Spain and San Fernando, and the industrial estates. The South, demarked by southerners as "all that land south of the Churchill-Roosevelt Highway" (just outside Port of Spain), represents, they say, 85 percent of the wealth of Trinidad. Mainly oil. The South, fiercely proud of its contribution to the national wealth and the national image, is experiencing some showers, blown from the Orinoco River in Venezuela, that will drench Port of Spain in the midafternoon.

Throughout the country nearly three hundred thousand (including nineteen hundred at the university) young Chinese, Indian, black, white faces sit down at their desks, conscious of Prime Minister Williams's emphasis on education. They know of the government's fifteen-year plan which began in 1964, and that it has more than doubled the number of secondary school students in the decade between 1962 and 1972; the aim: to provide junior secondary education to 90 percent of the eleven-years-plus age group and senior secondary education for approximately 40 percent of the fourteen-years-plus group. An emphasis on vocational and technical institutions has provided a chance to obtain qualifications that will help students get a job. Sixteen vocational schools are being built, each to accommodate 1,240 students, 440 day and 800 evening. Students also know that they have a chance for a long life ahead of them. Because of developments in the field of health, the death rate has declined to 6.8 per thousand—one of the lowest in the world; life expectancy increased from sixty-four years in 1960 to nearly seventy years by 1970. A large part of this is due to a greater understanding of how to cope with diseases or ailments such as polio, cholera, malaria (eradicated), influenza, respiratory diseases in children, typhoid, parasites, and yellow fever.

Throughout the day, schoolchildren visit their libraries, national, school, rural, and technical, to look into the past, prepare for the future. At the university's Kennedy Library (six floors, 120,000 books), a two-story window providing natural light, the room air-conditioned, a senior college student, seated in a bright aqua-blue easy chair, is intent on a volume from the section on Africa that he has selected from the stacks. He is researching the history of the Yorubas of West Africa, seeking, finding, and identifying cultural similarities with Trinidad's northeast coastal village of Toco. Another student, interested in science and botany,* is reviewing his notes from the previous day's visit to the Seismic Centre, which operates with British government assistance but is administratively part of the university. There had been four force-3 earthquakes in Trinidad during the past year and he is trying to calculate

---

* St. Augustine Campus, University of the West Indies, faculties: agriculture, engineering, arts and sciences, plus institutes of education and international relations and a computer center.

*The modern Kennedy Library at
the University of the West Indies*

when the next one will come. His interest in botany will take him over the weekend, in the company of an expert, to the Asa Wright Nature Centre, north of Arima (about forty minutes from the university). The center, a private organization, which receives local support as well as support from the United States, is rich in botanical specimens of the tropical rain forest. When there, he may also take the half-hour walk to see the oilbirds in their cave.

A small area is set aside on the fourth floor of the Kennedy Library for old books on Trinidad. Sitting at a desk in the enclosure, an undergraduate is reading into the past, researching the lives of persons who were born in Trinidad, and then had gone on to positions of note. Men like Eugene Chen, who later became foreign minister in China in the 1920s; George Padmore, the politician who was laid to final rest in Ghana; Learie Constantine, cricketer, politician, and lawyer, who became the first member of the British House of Lords of African descent; Stokely Carmichael, who created the Black Power slogan.

A group of citizens gathers at Woodford Square, in the center of downtown Port of Spain, which, like London's Hyde Park and New York City's Union Square, is a public forum for soapbox speeches. The group is only halfheartedly listening to a man speaking with rising voice and dramatic hand gestures. They are, in fact, discussing the prime minister's Best Village Trophy Competition. One man has the book *Patterns of Progress* in hand and is quoting from an article by Dr. J. D. Elder of the prime minister's office. He quotes: "The emphasis would be on Village-life, Folklore, Folk Arts, Folk Crafts, and Folk achievement in general. What is significant of this Project for students of national development is that it de-emphasised goal-orientation as an ideology and accentuated the crucial function of process-orientation in societies that are striving for advance." He says he feels that since Dr. Eric Williams had instituted the program in 1962, it might not have produced top talent, and certainly not a national theater, as in Jamaica, but it was most definitely serving its purpose. The Best Village Trophy Competition, like Carnival, perhaps more and in a different way, helps the people of Trinidad and Tobago find answers to their questions regarding unity.

Noontime. Lunchtime. Roti, a very special Trinidadian dish: meat wrapped in a pancake, on sale in restaurants, prepared in homes, purchased from mobile-van vendors. The noon breeze catches and transports the scent of roasted chataigne, lambie bouches, curried breadfruit chips, and grilled brego cakes. Port of Spain businessmen gather at the Union Club for relaxation or conference. A luncheon of ten in a hotel, friends entertaining a foreign visitor; a conversation drifting into a discussion of existing air services from North America to the Caribbean: Pan Am, BWIA, Air Canada, British Airways; also of LIAT's intra-Caribbean Service and Trinidad's Arawak Airline's run to Tobago. At the Queen's Park Hotel nearly sixty are seated in the semi-alfresco dining room at a periodic press corps luncheon. The doors of the visa section at the American embassy are still open, the waiting room packed. Today there is an average number of applicants—eighty; in summer the numbers for one day have been known to exceed three hundred. In 1972, seven thousand citizens applied for and were given visas for permanent residence in the United States, plus fifteen thousand more were given visitor visas.

Some drive to or through Federation Park, an attractive residential area. It, like other residential sections, has neat streets with sidewalks, houses close to one another, but each

*Trinidad's Parliament Building
in Port of Spain*

The start of the bicycle race
at Texaco's five-day Southern Games

with various degrees of privacy, high walls, lush trees, and gardens. The houses are mostly stucco, painted white; some are Spanish in flavor, with red-tiled roofs; a very few are of wood. In other parts of town stand the corrugated tin roofs over stucco, cinder block, or rough brick. Intricate second-floor window or roof fretwork in wood or iron is frequently found, particularly on older houses.

That afternoon a crowd of thirty thousand gathers at the Oval for a championship cricket match. This is the last day of the four-day match. The crowd goes wild after the break for tea and disperses as dusk sets in, delighted with the game, with their team's performance. The match was a draw.

Cricket is only one—though a very important—sport played by Trinidadians, who also enjoy basketball, rugby, soccer, table tennis, field hockey, netball, golf, lawn tennis, and badminton. Horseracing is extremely popular, with tracks in Port of Spain (the Savannah), San Fernando, Arima, and in Tobago, where goat races also take place at Easter time. There is legalized betting at horseraces; there is also national bingo and a national lottery. A major event of the sports year is Texaco's five-day Southern Games in March, which first began in 1938 and include foot races, high jump, javelin throw, shot put, broad jump, discus throw, rifle and pistol matches, and a great number of bicycle races, including the 15,000 meters.

While most Trinidadian men see the day through dressed in short-sleeved shirts, no tie, and trousers, businessmen in Port of Spain wear dark suits with jackets and ties. At sundown they change for the evening, either into another business suit or casual wear, which includes the increasingly popular shirt-jack, semitailored and comfortable tropical wear. Cocktail time, for those who can afford it, means scotch, the prestige drink, and for those who like it, the excellent local rum. Women, at receptions, dinners, or any evening event after 4 P.M., wear long dresses.

The steel bands can be heard practicing for Carnival—no matter what day of the year. A cruise ship lies lit at 4,400-foot King's Wharf; tourists have invaded tax-advantage shops strategically located near the ship on or just off Frederick Street. Most tourists by now are back on board; their ship is one of 1,600 oceangoing vessels that touch at Port of Spain annually. Perhaps on deck they look at the setting sun, with Venezuela clearly visible across the water.

Approximately 350,000 viewers watch the televised 7 P.M. evening news report. A short feature follows on labor union history and activity in Trinidad; it traces the origins of Labour Day (June 19), first celebrated in 1972, and the life of Tubal Uriah Buzz Butler, a national hero of the labor movement. Butler recalled June 19, 1937, when he led a march from Charlie King Corner, Fyzabad, in southern Trinidad, as the beginning of the industrial revolution. The 1937 strike in Trinidad's oil belt put Butler in the political limelight, and today the Oilfield Workers' Trade Union represents workers not only in two essential services—oil and electricity—but also in agriculture, construction, tire manufacturing, marine equipment, garment manufacturing, and entertainment. The Trinidad and Tobago Labour Congress (TTLC), associated with the Caribbean Congress of Labor (CCL), has within its association all unions not under or associated with the OWTU. The television report then turns to the weather prediction for tomorrow, same as today: "fair with showers."

Seventy-two cinemas throughout the country start their pro-

Horseracing is extremely popular in Trinidad and Tobago.

jectors; social and professional (including union) clubs open their doors to drinks, music, dance, and talk; a nightclub opens its doors with ear-shattering music; at one of the hotels, guests queue up for the weekly buffet of Trinidadian specialties: mangrove oysters, dolphin, calaloo soup.

The dogs start their nocturnal rounds; garbage-can lids are heard falling like cymbals. Trees become alive with chirps, squeaks, and a trill. Lizards venture from behind shutters or picture frames to crawl up a wall or across a ceiling in search of delicious bugs. Bats stretch their wings in the caves, drop into flight, and flap through the night. Giant six-foot turtles waddle onto the beaches to lay their eggs in the sand. Carnival costumes in the making hang on ropes under a backyard tin-roof shelter. Smoke rises from fields of burning sugarcane, sending a small glow skyward. A new mud island off the southern coast bubbles unseen to the surface. A guard stands watch on the pier at Staubles Bay, waves breaking gently against the white hulls of the four Coast Guard vessels. A senior government servant dreams of economic preferences, a subject on which he has been working all week. A few telephone calls pass through TEXTEL's switchboards to New York, Caracas, Bridgetown. Fourteen babies will be born before morning. And the oil continues to flow through the pipelines, the flared gas at Pointe-à-Pierre clearly visible from Port of Spain.

Carter, Herman. *West Indies.* Rev. ed. New York: Time-Life Books, 1966.

Cartey, Wilfred. *West Indies: Islands in the Sun.* Camden, N.J.: Thomas Nelson, Inc., 1967.

Evans, E. C. *First Geography of Trinidad and Tobago.* New York: Cambridge University Press, 1968.

Herskovits, Melville J., and Herskovits, Frances S. *Trinidad Village.* New York: Octagon Books, 1964.

Naipaul, V. S. *The Loss of El Dorado.* New York: Alfred A. Knopf, Inc., 1970.

Sherlock, Philip. *Land and People of the West Indies.* Philadelphia: J. B. Lippincott Co., 1967.

Williams, Eric. *From Columbus to Castro: The History of the Caribbean, 1492–1969.* New York: Harper & Row, Publishers, 1971.

————. *History of the People of Trinidad and Tobago.* Port of Spain, Trinidad: PNM Publishing Company, 1962.

SELECTED READING

INDEX

United Nations Conference on Trade and Development (UNCTAD), 42, 44

United Nations Industrial Development Organization (UNIDO), 42

United Nations University Council, 44

United States relations with Trinidad-Tobago. *See* Economics

Vialva, Isidore, 29

West Indies, University of the, 37, 50, 71

West Indies Federation, 31, 32, 39

Williams, Eric Eustace, 34, 37, 41, 44, 70, 74

Wooding, Hugh, 37

Anthony D. Marshall is a diplomat, businessman, author, and photographer who served as United States ambassador to Trinidad and Tobago. He has also been ambassador to the Malagasy Republic and now is in Africa again as ambassador to Kenya. He has written two other books, *The Malagasy Republic* and *Africa's Living Arts,* for Franklin Watts, Inc.

ABOUT THE AUTHOR